TAO
TE
CHING

TAO
TE
CHING

LAO TSU

TRANSLATED BY
GIA-FU FENG AND JANE ENGLISH

WITH AN INTRODUCTION AND NOTES
BY JACOB NEEDLEMAN

VINTAGE BOOKS
A DIVISION OF RANDOM HOUSE, INC.
NEW YORK

Vintage Books Edition, August 1989

Introduction and notes copyright © 1989 by Jacob Needleman
Copyright © 1972 by Gia-fu Feng and Jane English

Library of Congress Cataloging-in-Publication Data

Lao-tsu.
    [Tao te ching. English]
    Tao te ching/Lao-tsu; translated by Gia-fu Feng and Jane
English; with an introduction and notes by Jacob Needleman.
— 1st Vintage Books ed.
    p. cm.
    Originally published: New York: Knopf, 1972.
    ISBN 0-679-72434-6: $6.95
    I. English, Jane. II. Feng, Gia-Fu. III. Title.
BL1900.L3E5 1989
299'.51482—dc19   89-45146
                                              CIP

Manufactured in the United States of America
3579C864

INTRODUCTION

The eighty-one short chapters known as the *Tao Te Ching* have been translated more often than any other book in the world, with the single exception of the Bible. Like the Bible, the *Tao Te Ching* is a book whose appeal is as broad as its meaning is deep. It speaks to each of us at our own level of understanding, while inviting us to search for levels of insight and experience that are not yet within our comprehension. As with every text that deserves to be called sacred, it is a half-silvered mirror. To read it is not only to see ourselves as we are but to glimpse a greatness extending far beyond our knowledge of ourselves and the universe we live in.

"The Tao that can be told is not the eternal Tao": These words are among the most famous in all the literature of the world. They were first offered, however, not to modern, Western people like ourselves who, approaching the twenty-first century, are ready to admit that we have given too much place to discursive thought and rationalism. They were spoken some 2,500 years ago to a people and in a place, ancient China, far, far removed from us. Any work of art that communicates so enduringly over such enormous reaches of time and cultural diversity addresses, we may be sure, the essence of human nature and the human condition, rather than sociocultural aspects that are peculiar to this or that society. The *Tao Te Ching* deals with what is *permanent* in us. It speaks of a possible inner greatness and an equally possible inner failure, which are both indelibly written into our very structure as human beings. Under its gaze, we are not "American" or "Chinese" or "European." We are that being, Man, uniquely called to occupy a precise place in the cosmic order, no matter where or in what era we live.

The *Tao Te Ching* is thus a work of metaphysical psychology, taking us far beyond the social or biological factors that have been the main concern of modern psychology. It helps us see how the fundamental forces of the cosmos itself are mirrored in our own individual, inner structure. And it invites us to try to live in direct relationship to all these forces. To see truly and to live fully: this is what it means to be authentically human. But it is extremely challenging and this challenge was apparently as difficult for the men and women of ancient China as it is for us. We too try in vain to live full lives without understanding what it means to *see*. We too presume to act, to do, to create, without opening ourselves to a vision of ultimate reality. This opening and the way to experience it are what the *Tao Te Ching* is about.

Historical information about the text and its author is scant and cloaked in legend. Even the little information we have is at every point subject to dispute by scholars, although many are willing to accept that Lao Tsu was a real person born in what is now known as the Honan province in China some six centuries before the Christian era. Tradition has it that Confucius once journeyed to see Lao Tsu and came away amazed and in awe of the man. According to the tale, Confucius described his meeting with Lao Tsu in the following way: "I know a bird can fly, a fish can swim, an animal can run. For that which runs a net can be made; for that which swims a line can be made; for that which flies a corded arrow can be made. But the dragon's ascent into heaven on the wind and the clouds is something which is beyond my knowledge. Today I have seen Lao Tsu who is perhaps like a dragon."[1]

The tale also tells that Lao Tsu was the keeper of the imperial archives at the ancient capital of Loyang. Seeing the imminent decay of the society he lived in, he resolved to ride away alone into the desert. But at the Han-ku Pass he was stopped by a gatekeeper named Yin Hsi, who knew of his reputation for wisdom and who begged him to set down in writing the essence of his teaching. Thus, the legend tells us, the *Tao Te Ching* came into being.

Legend aside, there is no doubt about the immense importance of this text in the history of China and the Orient. The figure of Lao Tsu and his writings are revered by followers of the Taoist religion, and the message of the *Tao Te Ching* has been one of the major underlying influences in Chinese thought and culture for more than two thousand years. Throughout the world, when one thinks of the greatest spiritual figures in the history of mankind, Lao Tsu is placed alongside Christ, Gautama Buddha, Moses, and Mohammed.

[1] Quoted in D. C. Lau, *Tao Te Ching* (Harmondsworth, England: Penguin Books, 1963), 8.

Some remarks about the language of this work may be of help at this point. The word *Tao* (pronounced "dow") has been characterized as untranslatable by nearly every modern scholar. But this statement should not lead us to imagine that the meaning of the Tao was any more easily understood by the contemporaries of Lao Tsu. It would be more to the point to say, only half jokingly, that the word *Tao*, and even the whole of the *Tao Te Ching*, is not readily translatable into any language, including Chinese! "My words are easy to understand and easy to perform," wrote Lao Tsu, "yet no man under heaven knows them or practices them" (Ch. 70).

The present translation generally leaves the word *Tao* in Chinese. Those who have sought an equivalent in Western languages have almost invariably settled on *Way* or *Path*. Metaphysically, the term *Tao* refers to the way things are; psychologically, it refers to the way human nature is constituted, the deep, dynamic structure of our being; ethically, it means the way human beings must conduct themselves with others; spiritually, it refers to the guidance that is offered to us, the methods of searching for the truth that have been handed down by the great sages of the past — the way of inner work. Yet all these meanings of *Tao* are ultimately one. In this work we are offered a vision that relates the flowing structure of the universe to the structure of our individual nature, both in itself and as it manifests in the details of our everyday actions in the world.

No linguistic or philosophic analysis of this word can ever capture its essential meaning, because what is being referred to is an experience that can be understood only at the moment it is "tasted" with the whole of our being — simultaneously sensed, felt, and thought; and because this way of experiencing is entirely different from the way almost all of us act and think and feel in our usual lives.

To say that the realization of metaphysical truth lies in the opposite direction from the way we usually experience our lives is not to say that a different "method" of thinking or experiencing is required. What is at issue is nothing less than the activation of an entirely new power within us, an entirely new movement of consciousness. The point is that man is built to receive, contain, and transform this power and then to make his life a complete expression of it. Nothing else can bring ultimate fulfillment into human life. And yet our lives are lived with little awareness or contact with this force of consciousness. We work, we love, we struggle, we eat, sleep, and dream, we write books and create art, we even worship our gods closed off from it. This is why every sacred teaching in the history of mankind begins as a revolution — incomprehensible, paradoxical, mysterious. Whether it be the gnomic teaching of Lao Tsu — whoever he was and *if* he was — or the profoundly troubling doctrine of un-knowing brought by Socrates, or the exalted, hidden God speaking through Moses and the prophets of Israel, or the shattering sacrifice of love transmitted by Jesus, every sacred teaching remains sacred only as long as it opens a path that has never before been opened and yet always exists and must always exist for humanity.

> Look, it cannot be seen — it is beyond form.
> Listen, it cannot be heard — it is beyond sound.
> Grasp, it cannot be held — it is intangible.

. . . .
It is called indefinable and beyond imagination.
Stand before it and there is no beginning.
Follow it and there is no end.
Stay with the ancient Tao,
Move with the present.

(Ch. 14)

Of equal importance in approaching this text, and the life it
calls us to, is the word *Te* (pronounced "deh"). This word directs
our attention to the question of the expression or manifestation
in our day-to-day lives of the supreme reality. The present text,
following numerous other translations, renders *Te* by the English word *Virtue*. But we must be careful not to bring our ordinary
moralistic associations to this term. It is true that the
word *Te* introduces us to the ethical dimension of this teaching,
but this is ethics that is solidly rooted in metaphysics, and
completely separate from ethics considered as the rules of social
morality, which vary from culture to culture, epoch to epoch,
nation to nation, class to class. *Te* refers to nothing less than the
quality of human action that allows the central, creative power
of the universe to manifest through it.

Something mysteriously formed,
Born before heaven and earth.
In the silence and the void,
Standing alone and unchanging,
Ever present and in motion.
Perhaps it is the mother of ten thousand things.
I do not know its name.
Call it Tao.
For lack of a better word, I call it great.

Being great, it flows.
It flows far away.
Having gone far, it returns.

Therefore, "Tao is great;
Heaven is great;
Earth is great;
The king is also great."
These are the four great powers of the universe,
And the king is one of them.

Man follows the earth.
Earth follows heaven.
Heaven follows the Tao.
Tao follows what is natural.
(Ch. 25)

The picture before us is of a cosmic force or principle that expands or flows outward or, more precisely perhaps, descends into the creation of the universe, "the ten thousand things." Together with this, we are told of a force or movement of return. All of creation returns to the source. But the initial coming-into-being of creation is to be understood as a receiving of that which flows downward and outward from the center. Every created entity ultimately is what it is and does what it does owing to its specific reception of the energy radiating from the ultimate, formless reality. This movement from the nameless Source to the ten thousand things is *Te*. And the unique being, man, called here the *king*, is created to receive this force consciously and is called to allow his actions to manifest that force. Such conscious receiving in human life is Virtue. Thus, the movement that leads back toward the Source is also the opening toward great action in outer life. Virtue is an opening rather than a "doing."

In sum, Lao Tsu distinguished human Virtue from what we ordinarily consider moral action by the cosmic nature of the force that human Virtue manifests. Great action, for Lao Tsu, is action that conducts the highest and subtlest conscious energy. Ordinary moral action is, on the contrary, a manifestation whose source is "lower down" in the vast chain of being as it is portrayed in chapter 25: Tao, heaven, earth, the king (or man). The ego, our ordinary "initiator of action," is an ephemeral construction, which is formed by factors operating far beneath the level of the Source and which, in the unenlightened state of awareness, represents a kind of blockage or impediment to the interplay of fundamental cosmic forces. In other words, because of our identification of ourselves with the ego, what we ordinarily call action, or "doing," in fact cuts us off from the complete reception of conscious energy in our bodies and actions.

This idea must inevitably sound revolutionary, overthrowing the value we place on socially constructed systems of morality and efficiency. For the point is not only *what* we do but the source from which we do it. The metaphysical nature of that source determines the ethical, cognitive, and pragmatic value of all human action — that is, the goodness, truth, and practicality of what we do in our life on earth. Our primary and perhaps only true responsibility is to become individuals who are also conduits for the supreme creative power of the universe. All other responsibilities — for knowing the truth, for feeling the good, and for accomplishing what is useful and effective — must flow from this: in our external world, in our day-to-day lives, and within the recesses of our psychological makeup. In the ancient traditions of the West, this idea has been known as the doctrine of man as microcosm. In Christian and Jewish mysticism, in the philosophy of Plato and the Hermetic tradition, in Islamic esotericism, we find this idea pouring forth in an endless symphony of symbolic forms and profoundly articulated ideas. In the *Tao Te Ching* it is offered to us as a whisper.

Thus:

Respect of Tao and honor of Virtue are not demanded.
But they are in the nature of things.

Therefore all things arise from Tao.
By Virtue they are nourished,
Developed, cared for,
Sheltered, comforted,
Grown and protected.
Creating without claiming,
Doing without taking credit,
Guiding without interfering,
This is Primal Virtue.

(Ch. 51)

We are now in a position to consider what for many of us is the most compelling aspect of the *Tao Te Ching*, namely, the putting into practice of its teaching. The metaphysical doctrine now stands before us in outline: an unformed, ungraspable, pure conscious principle lies at the heart and origin of all things; it is referred to as the *Tao*. This principle moves, expands, descends into form, creating the hierarchically, organically ordered cascade of worlds and phenomena called "the ten thousand things," or simply the great universe — and this movement, especially as it can move through humanity, is called *Te*, Virtue. At the same time, there is a great tide of return to the source, back toward the undifferentiated, pure reality of the "uncarved block." This movement is also termed *Tao*. Finally, the supreme whole comprised of both movements is also given the designation *Tao*. (*Ching*, by the way, simply means *book*.)

Man is built to be an individual incarnation of this whole. His good, his happiness — the very meaning of his life — is to live in correspondence and relationship to the whole, to be and act precisely as the universe itself is and moves. The question before us now is *how?* The *Tao Te Ching* offers a powerful and practical answer, describing in almost every chapter this way of living, also known as *Tao*, the Way.

The secret of living, according to the *Tao Te Ching*, is to open within ourselves to the great flow of fundamental forces that constitute the ultimate nature of the universe — both the movement that descends from the source *and* the movement of return.

Empty yourself of everything.
Let the mind become still.
The ten thousand things rise and fall while the Self watches
   their return.
They grow and flourish and then return to the source.
   Returning to the source is stillness, which is the way
   of nature.

                                                                    (Ch. 16)

Expressions like this show us why the *Tao Te Ching* has assumed such great popularity at the present moment. There is a widely shared realization that modern man has arrogantly and foolishly believed in science, a product largely of the intellect alone and not of the whole man, as an instrument for imposing his will upon nature. And, in the relationships among peoples, Europeans and Americans have often assumed the right to impose their values and desires upon peoples whose lives have not yet based themselves on the technological applications of science. As for Western religion, the Judeo-Christian tradition has sometimes been perceived, rightly or wrongly, as supporting this general tendency in the psychological sphere, especially insofar as it presents a fierce moral demand, a commandment that the individual override his own instinctive, emotional nature, and conform his life to standards that suffocate the vital forces within the body and the heart of every human being.

There is nothing new in this reaction against what is perceived as the tyranny of an intellectualist and puritanical value system. Our culture heard it in the early criticism of the Industrial Revolution — in the work of Blake, Dostoyevsky, Kierkegaard, and Nietzsche, to name only a few. The first half of the twentieth century has seen aspects of it in the psychoanalytic movement, which sought to open our awareness to the forces of organic nature within us, and in the writings of the existentialists, who called for the recognition of a radical inner freedom unfixed and undetermined by any laws, cosmic or societal. Finally, in recent years we have witnessed the growing interest in mysticism and Eastern religion, which, despite some highly publicized bizarre concomitants, has introduced powerful new ideas into the currents of Western thought; chief among them, perhaps, is the idea of the states of human consciousness and the suggestion that the whole of our lives, individually and collectively, proceeds in a diminished state of consciousness, far from the capacities that would be possible were we to live at the level of consciousness that is natural to us.

It is this last claim that can sound a truly new note for most people and that provides the context in which the *Tao Te Ching* can speak in a stunning, fresh way about the practical question of how to search and how to live. Once the immensity of the idea of levels of consciousness is felt, the message of the *Tao Te Ching* soars beyond social and philosophical criticism of our culture. We find ourselves in front of a teaching about nature and naturalness that compels us to see even our very legitimate current concerns about the environment and our planet in a way that is far more immediate and at the same time far more inclusive than we might ever have imagined. And we shall see that the same holds true for other urgent issues of our time, including the problem of war, the crisis of leadership, and the man-woman relationship.

To understand the practical importance of the idea of nature and naturalness contained in the *Tao Te Ching,* there is perhaps no better place to start than with the phrase that has become such a part of our contemporary vocabulary that it has assumed the status of a cliché and even a joke: "to go with the flow." Do these words in their popular use mean the same thing as living according to the Tao? Certainly not. The distortions of this phrase that have become popular suggest an unthinking passivity along with a naive trust in the flow of outer events. But it is also a distortion to equate the ideal of living in accord with the Tao with simply obeying one's inner emotional and physical desires, as well as one's hidden intellectual prejudices. The point here is well illustrated by an exchange between the Zen master Shunryu Suzuki and his American pupils:

> There is a big misunderstanding about the idea of naturalness. Most people who come to us believe in some freedom or naturalness, but their understanding is what we call *jinen ken gedo*, or heretical naturalness. . . a kind of "let-alone policy" or sloppiness. . . For a plant or stone to be natural is no problem. But for us there is some problem, indeed a big problem. To be natural is something we must work on.[2]

Suzuki's further comments lead us to consider the ideas of non-being *(wu)* and non-action *(wu-wei)*, which are central to the practical teaching of the *Tao Te Ching*. He goes on to speak of *nyu nan shin*, a "smooth, natural mind":

> When you have that, you have the joy of life. When you lose it, you lose everything. You have nothing. Although you think you have something, you have nothing. But when all you do comes out of nothingness, then you have everything. . . . That is what we mean by naturalness.[3]

In the words of Lao Tsu:

> Tao abides in non-action,
> Yet nothing is left undone.

[2] Shunryu Suzuki, *Zen Mind, Beginner's Mind* (New York and Tokyo: Weatherhill, 1970), 105-6.
[3] Ibid., 106.

If kings and lords observed this,
The ten thousand things would develop naturally.
If they still desired to act,
They would return to the simplicity of formless substance.

(Ch. 37)

To be natural, therefore, is not easy. Inwardly, it involves a state of openness or receptivity that is subtle, elusive, and *active*. It means becoming aware of that supreme creative power which, as has been said, human beings were created to contain and express. Or, from another angle, one might equally say that to be natural is easy, but we have become such unnatural beings that to be open to this force is the most difficult thing in the world. It requires of us an effort that is wholly unlike anything we understand as effort, even including what is ordinarily called "relaxation."

Similarly, our understanding of nature as an external reality invites reconsideration. Our perception of nature is relative to the quality of mind or attention that serves as our instrument of cognition. We see only things, entities, events; we do not directly experience the forces and laws that govern nature and the cosmos.

Ever desireless, one can see the mystery.
Ever desiring, one sees the manifestations.

(Ch. 1)

Let us note: A mind governed by desires can perceive only the world of appearances. What exists behind these appearances can be known only by the mind that exists behind the desires in ourselves.

Let us further note: Just as the universe contains "the ten

thousand things" — creatures, worlds, stars, stones — so does our mind contain its own "ten thousand things," namely, desires, impulses, fears, and sensations, and the thoughts, logically connected or not, that serve them.

Thus a mind that is full of content knows a universe that is full of things. To go behind the apparent universe requires that we go behind the apparent mind. This may be called "opening to non-being." At the same time, what Lao Tsu called *non-being* is a force of irresistible, ultimate power. It is most certainly not "nothing" in the usual sense of that word. Nor is it "existence" in the usual sense of the word. Similarly, for ourselves: What lies beneath the glittering surface of our mind or ordinary sense of self are not simply other fabulous "things," such as the psychological "black holes" that modern psychology has revealed to us under the designation of the "unconscious."

What lies behind "the ten thousand things" — or, to use Western language, behind the appearances in ourselves and in the universe — is not another world, another "thing" or collection of "things." Not new stars, planets, or black holes; not new desires, sensations, or insights. What lies behind the ten thousand things is the awareness of the ten thousand things. What lies behind the ego is the awareness of the ego. But this awareness — what is it? We cannot say. Call it Tao. The "other world," the "real world" out there and in here is *simply* this world illumined with the inconceivably powerful and subtle energy of consciousness — which we perhaps are beginning to recognize as love itself.

Love — our Western civilization has always needed that word and no doubt still needs it. Speaking against those who would reduce the great Judaic revelation to a system of formal commandments, external demands, and legalistic rulings, the prophets of Israel arose as the hidden voice of conscience conducting the message of inwardness to the feelings of a nation. The shock of the prophetic voice was continually covered over by fear and egoism and the thinking that served these weaknesses. "My thoughts are not your thoughts," God tells Israel through the prophet Isaiah (55:8). "I hate, I despise your feast days," God tells Israel through Amos (5:21). Again and again God calls on Israel to open inwardly to the ultimate mystery that sends its love continuously toward humanity and through humanity to the world we are meant to live in, what we call "earth." And throughout centuries what we clumsily call "Jewish mysticism" speaks only of the need for humanity to receive, to open, to become "like a woman" toward the "fatherhood" of the ultimate mystery.

Following the great line of prophets, there then appeared another prophet, or was he more than a prophet? Again, but with the unfathomable newness, gentleness, and power of the highest energy, the message of love is given. And a life is lived, a death is lived on the cross, the shattering reverberations of which are still unfolding in our world. A sacrifice is offered, a gift is given, and humanity is confronted with the grievous truth that we are unable to accept that gift. We must work and struggle, with a kind of effort totally new and unknown, to receive the gift in the tissues of our being. We must set aside all that tense *doing* we call action. We must become *female,* just as creation itself arises as the mother of the ten thousand things.

> The nameless is the beginning of heaven and earth.
> The named is the mother of ten thousand things.
>
> (Ch. 1)

Female is all that receives and brings to birth. We are built to receive all the energies of creation in our consciousness and, through the mysterious activity of watchful silence, to allow them to gestate and unfold in the fullness of time.

> A great country is like low land.
> It is the meeting ground of the universe,
> The mother of the universe.
> The female overcomes the male with stillness,
> Lying low in stillness.
>
> (Ch. 61)

> The valley spirit never dies;
> It is the woman, primal mother.
> Her gateway is the root of heaven and earth.
> It is like a veil barely seen.
> Use it; it will never fail.
>
> (Ch. 6)

Lao Tsu's teaching about "the female" is bound to be of great interest in contemporary culture. However, there is no question here of direct application to any social or political issue having to do with the rights of women. It is purely and solely a question of the nature of human-ness itself. What is a human being — *anterior* to the division into man and woman? The point is that a human being can only act, that is, move outward, in a manner that is specifically human, to the extent that he or she can receive the gift of energy being poured out from the source. We are destined to be beings in which the primal two are in conscious, harmonious relationship. We are beings of two movements. It is our exalted but immensely difficult task to find the sensitivity and openness that is the great movement of return designated by the

word *silence* at the same time that we function outwardly —
think, play, fight, and create — in the rough-and-tumble vortex
of life on earth. The *male* moves out, the *female* returns;
the *male* speaks, the *female* is silent; the *male* knows, the *female* is.
That is to say, our speech must be rooted in silence; our
movement must be permeated by stillness.

> Carrying body and soul and embracing the one,
> Can you avoid separation?
> .   .   .   .
> Opening and closing the gates of heaven,
> Can you play the role of woman?
>   (Ch. 10)

There is a tendency in some contemporary scholarship to offer
modernistic psychological and political reasons for the prejudice
against women in the history of religion and culture throughout
the world. No doubt these speculations are valid in many cases
and at their level. But insofar as the female designates a universal,
metaphysical energy, the movement of opening and return, it is
simply inevitable that the female becomes *that which is forgotten*, that
which is *not understood*. Inevitable, that is, granted the "fallen"
nature of humanity, our disconnection from the authentic
possibilities of our life.

In the ancient Chinese idea of *yin* and *yang*,[4] *yin* is associated
with ideas of the female as darkness, death, dissolution —
everything that is complementary to *yang* as male, bright,
creational, outpouring. No greater mistake can be made than to

[4] The idea is ancient, but the symbol of the circle divided into black
and white dates from tenth-century neo-Confucianism.

equate the female with mere "emotions" or so-called intuition. The emotional function in unenlightened men and women — in us — is as little open to the higher as the actional function in unenlightened individuals is an outward *expression* of the higher creative energy. The creation pours down in light and in accordance with rigorous laws of unfolding. It is uncompromising in its action, and it does not "care" for things in a manner that follows our limited and egoistically fantastic standards.

> Heaven and earth are impartial;
> They see the ten thousand things as straw dogs.
>   (Ch. 5)

Similarly, no greater mistake can be made than to equate the male, the positive, active force of the cosmos with mere thinking or so-called rationality. Thus, *yin* accords as little with historically conditioned concepts of the feminine as *yang* accords with historically conditioned concepts of the masculine.

Seen in this way, both the male and the female force are hidden from us in our unenlightened state of consciousness. It requires a precise practice of meditation to become aware of energies as such, and to observe for oneself the laws of their interaction and unfolding movement. This inner practice reveals that all phenomena everywhere depend upon the harmonious relationship of these forces called *yin* and *yang*, female and male, return and expression. To be fully human is to develop a power of attention that allows this relationship to take place within one's own psychophysical organism. A man in whom this attention is highly developed is called a sage, an enlightened human being —

although here too there are levels and degrees of inner attainment.

As has been suggested, the study that leads to the emergence of this consciousness within ourselves is known as the path, *Tao* understood as the Way of inner spiritual practice. We have just introduced the term "meditation." Setting aside most contemporary meanings of this word, we may characterize meditation as the process of becoming familiar with one's own real structure as a human being. Certain definite conditions, such as physical posture and mental attitude, have in every spiritual tradition been presented as necessary supports for this process. The *Tao Te Ching* does not offer this kind of advice, apart from the mental attitude so powerfully communicated by the text. In fact, the most important features of the "technical" aspect of meditation can never be written down. The practice of meditation requires direct personal guidance of an exceedingly delicate sort, and as such constitutes a central aspect of the vast and all-important element of spiritual discipline known as the oral transmission. All effective spiritual transmission ultimately takes place directly between people. It can never be learned from a book.

But important general and theoretical aspects of the practice *can* be expressed in words and images, and so, returning to the point at hand, we can say that one of the first truths discovered in the practice of meditation is that the movement of return, the movement back toward one's central self, is a subtle, elusive, and fleeting experience. It is constantly being overridden by the automatically acting aspects of the outward movement, especially the racing chaos of automatic thoughts. Even more subtle and elusive, yet of cardinal importance, is the experience of both forces together within oneself. The metaphysical symbol of this central experience is the yin-yang diagram as a whole. That experience is the knowledge and incarnation of the *Tao* considered as the whole, of nature and of oneself as the whole.

It is not the intention of this introduction to try to say more about such subtle experiences but to focus on general, theoretical aspects and implications.

Nor is it the intention to try to introduce the teaching of the *Tao Te Ching* in the form of a system of philosophy. The chapters of the text are interrelated; but, as with every communication from a higher level of spirituality, the interrelation appears to us as replete with contradictions and disconnected images. There is bound to be confusion in our minds about the meanings of *yin* and *yang*, and about which sense of the Tao is being referred to in many of the chapters. We can say, however, that one stage of the work of meditation is to discriminate between the two forces, the movement of return and the movement outward. Another stage, presupposing the experience of successive discrimination, is the simultaneous experience of both; a third stage would then be the experience of the moving together into a harmonious relationship of these two forces. That further stages exist there can be no doubt. But it is also certain that we are not in a position to speculate about them.

At every stage of the practice, the truth one needs to experience is *hidden* and dark, and bears the marks of *death*. This is the death of all that has been built up by the automatism of the mind and ego. It is the death of forms and the momentary release or appearance of a formless energy. The seeker must allow himself or herself to be the female in relation to that which is waiting to pour itself into the seeker from above — whether it be called truth or the ultimate energy.

> Yield and overcome;
> Bend and be straight;
> Empty and be full;
> Wear out and be new;
> Have little and gain;
> Have much and be confused.
>   (Ch. 22)

> Know the strength of man,
> But keep a woman's care!
>   .   .   .   .
> Know the white,
> But keep the black!
>   .   .   .   .
> Be the valley of the universe!
> Being the valley of the universe,
> Ever true and resourceful,
> Return to the state of the uncarved block.
>   (Ch. 28)

The psychological condition of an individual who seeks in this way to experience both fundamental forces in himself must inevitably appear incomprehensible and even foolish to the unenlightened — and to the unenlightened parts of our own minds, which are accustomed, one might even say addicted, to "rationality" and the imposition of concepts and forms onto the outer and inner life.

But I alone am drifting, not knowing where I am.
Like a newborn babe before it learns to smile,
I am alone, without a place to go.

Others have more than they need, but I alone have nothing.
I am a fool. Oh, yes! I am confused.
Other men are clear and bright,
But I alone am dim and weak.
Other men are sharp and clever,
But I alone am dull and stupid.
Oh, I drift like the waves of the sea,
Without direction, like the restless wind.
Everyone else is busy, But I alone am aimless and depressed.
I am different
I am nourished by the great mother.

(Ch. 20)

Hence it is said:
The bright path seems dim;
Going forward seems like retreat;
The easy way seems hard;
The highest Virtue seems empty;

.   .   .   .

The greatest form has no shape.
The Tao is hidden and without name,
The Tao alone nourishes and brings everything to fulfillment.

(Ch. 41)

We may now consider the numerous verses of the *Tao Te Ching* that deal with the question of leadership, political and spiritual. Before citing examples, we need to emphasize the extraordinary difficulty and drama that awaits the individual seeking to embrace the *yin* and *yang* within himself. It is not for nothing that in the spiritual language of alchemy this embrace, under the name "alchemical marriage" or the "divine androgyne," is presented as the culmination of long and difficult work on oneself. It is a question of developing an attention of such strength and sensitivity that two fundamental cosmic forces, which on one level are intrinsically at war with each other, come together under an even greater force of reconciliation. War is transmuted into love. This reference to the language of Western alchemy may help us confront the political and military language that enters in the second part of the *Tao Te Ching*. Otherwise, it may be hopelessly puzzling that a text which so consistently speaks of gentleness and yielding suddenly begins speaking of warfare, generalship, armies, and military strategy. This aspect of the *Tao Te Ching* has led some modern interpreters to take it as a blueprint for achieving purposes completely alien to the goal of inner freedom — such as military conquest or even effective business management and sales programs!

In any case, the *Tao Te Ching* does speak of struggle and discipline quite as much as it speaks of non-doing and letting go, as in fact do all the inner disciplines of the great spiritual teachings, East and West. It is an extraordinary task to make conscious contact with the energy that reconciles the two great movements of universal reality at the levels in which they operate within the whole of the human psyche.

The exalted vision that has revealed the necessity for this "in between" state is surely what lies at the heart of the *Middle* Way as it originally took form in the teaching of the Buddha. The same vision informs the esoteric Christianity of Meister Eckhardt; the fathers of Byzantine Christianity, such as Gregory Palamas and Maximus the Confessor; and the Gnostic texts of early Christianity. It is the vision we find in the Jewish mystical writings known as the Zohar and the stories of the Baal Shem Tov and his spiritual descendants. It is, as was said, the central work of alchemy. It is Arjuna's "warfare" in the *Bhagavad Gita,* the "spiritual combat" of the *Philokalia,* the Zen Buddhist "Sword of the Mind," the way of the "warrior" as spoken of by Hakuin.

To see the Tao's message as a permissive, passive, self-calming "going with the flow" in the way some modern writers have is to make a mere fantasy out of a profound, subtle doctrine that blends into one vision the truth of Mercy and the truth of Rigor, to use the language of the Kabbalah. To make *non-doing* into non-struggling is to be an advocate of what has become merely one of the world's great half-truths.

It is possible to understand this teaching concerning the inbetweenness of inner freedom as lying at the root of the Western doctrines of moderation and sobriety that we find in the philosophers of ancient Greece and Rome. But when we consider the way this Western idea has come down to us, it too must be seen as a degeneration, insofar as it directs us toward a kind of "bourgeois" metaphysics and psychology. "Nothing in excess," as the Greeks and Romans expressed it, cannot at its root mean anything like the existential comfortableness or puritanism it has come to signify. It must have originally emerged out of the same kind of doctrine we find in the *Tao Te Ching* and the countless other esoteric spiritual teachings of the world: namely, to struggle for an attention or consciousness that can embrace two opposite forces without being swallowed by either. It means living in the midst of both the forces of outer life and the forces of the mystical return while searching in oneself for the consciousness that is at the root and that stands as the reconciling fulfillment of both these movements. This war is love. This love is war.

In the light of these comments, we can now look at what our text tells us about the art of living in the world, and especially the practical art of leadership — what Plato spoke of both symbolically and literally as "statesmanship." The question is, how to live one's daily life in a way that supports and expresses this war of love, this struggle for contact with the transcendently vibrant non-being, emptiness, and formless energy that lies at the heart of the human and the cosmic world.

Surely the following verses, and those like them in the text, tell us something essential about how to govern and how to fight. The historic context of ancient Chinese society — its political strife and social unrest — cannot be ignored. But we must ask ourselves: to what extent do these verses teach us about how to achieve success in the forms by which society enables us to deal with each other, and to what extent do they give us an attitude toward these forms that enables us to seek within while we are compelled to move and act in the social context? To what extent are spiritual principles meant to serve social-psychological goals, and to what extent can social activity become the milieu in which we search for that which transcends "society"? Do we meditate in order to win? Or can we study the laws of pure inner work operating even within the outer battlefield of life?

Therefore the stiff and unbending is the disciple of death.
The gentle and yielding is the disciple of life.

Thus an army without flexibility never wins a battle.
A tree that is unbending is easily broken.
The hard and strong will fall.
The soft and weak will overcome.

(Ch. 76)

People usually fail when they are on the verge of success.
So give as much care to the end as to the beginning;
Then there will be no failure.
Therefore the sage seeks freedom from desire.
He does not collect precious things.
He learns not to hold on to ideas.
He brings men back to what they have lost.
He helps the ten thousand things find their own nature,
But refrains from action.

(Ch. 64)

In the symbolic language of sacred writing, the outer and the inner are spoken of with images and formulations that embrace the laws of one's own inner world and the great outer world simultaneously. In this language, words such as *leader, warrior, king,* and *sage* refer both to an individual in relationship to other people and to a part of oneself in its relationship to the other parts that make up one's total inner world. There is or can be a leader in myself — a warrior, king, and sage. There are armies and peoples within myself. There are desires, fears, hopes, needs; there are timid and brave impulses; there are thinkers, dreamers, scoundrels, and madmen. In the Old Testament these are "the people of Israel" whom Moses leads out of the state of slavery.

These are the "people" of Plato's Republic, whom the philosopher-king rules with wisdom and justice. Like the *Tao Te Ching*, such texts are "political" in a much vaster and more intimate sense than we may imagine. To be a warrior in the outer life, one must be a warrior in the inner life. To be a king in the outer life, one must be a king in the inner life. To be a sage in the outer life, one must be a sage in the inner life.

Thus, when the *Tao Te Ching* cautions the ruler against imposing concepts of good and evil onto his people, it is also cautioning us against cutting ourselves off from the vital forces within ourselves through attachment to mental or emotional judging of ourselves. To read anything in the *Tao Te Ching* as merely advice for the outer life is, putting it bluntly, to desecrate it, that is, to pack it into our own store of illusions, the sum total of which has made our individual and collective life on earth a hypnotic sleep that could very well end with our eyes still closed. But to read it as applying simultaneously to the outer life and to our own inner life is to feel ourselves invited to a life of searching that will be supported by the strongest and greatest energies in the universe.

—*Jacob Needleman*

I wish to acknowledge with gratitude the help I have received in presenting this introduction to the *Tao Te Ching*. Dr. Ronald Epstein of the Philosophy Department at San Francisco State University made many sensitive and illuminating suggestions based not only on his extensive scholarly expertise in the Chinese language and culture but also on his own considerable personal experience with the realities of religion. I am also deeply grateful to my great friend and editor at Alfred A. Knopf, Toinette Lippe, for inviting me to introduce, edit, and provide notes for this new edition of this much loved translation. Her advice and criticism not only on this manuscript but over the years has been an irreplaceable gift to me. It should be noted that some of the most distinguished spiritual texts and translations that have appeared in English over the past two decades owe an immense amount to her.

As for other translations of the *Tao Te Ching* that have been of help to me, they are listed in the selected bibliography at the end of the book. Many of these volumes also contain insightful commentaries. Of commentaries that stand alone without being joined to translations of the complete text, I wish to mention two that have proved very valuable to me: *A Comparative Study of the Key Philosophical Concepts in Sufism and Taoism*, by Toshihiko Izutsu (Tokyo: Keio Institute in Cultural and Linguistic Studies, 1967), and an unpublished work, *Tao Te Ching: The Wisdom of Lao Tzu*, by David Stollar.

TAO
TE
CHING

ONE

The Tao that can be told is not the eternal Tao.
The name that can be named is not the eternal name.
The nameless is the beginning of heaven and earth.
The named is the mother of ten thousand things.
Ever desireless, one can see the mystery.
Ever desiring, one sees the manifestations.
These two spring from the same source but differ in name;
    this appears as darkness.
Darkness within darkness.
The gate to all mystery.

TWO

Under heaven all can see beauty as beauty only because
  there is ugliness.
All can know good as good only because there is evil.

Therefore having and not having arise together.
Difficult and easy complement each other.
Long and short contrast each other;
High and low rest upon each other;
Voice and sound harmonize each other;
Front and back follow one another.

Therefore the sage goes about doing nothing, teaching
  no-talking.
The ten thousand things rise and fall without cease,
Creating, yet not possessing,
Working, yet not taking credit.
Work is done, then forgotten.
Therefore it lasts forever.

THREE

Not exalting the gifted prevents quarreling.
Not collecting treasures prevents stealing.
Not seeing desirable things prevents confusion of the heart.

The wise therefore rule by emptying hearts and stuffing
    bellies, by weakening ambitions and strengthening bones.
If men lack knowledge and desire, then clever people will not
    try to interfere.
If nothing is done, then all will be well.

FOUR

The Tao is an empty vessel; it is used, but never filled.
Oh, unfathomable source of ten thousand things!
Blunt the sharpness,
Untangle the knot,
Soften the glare,
Merge with dust.
Oh, hidden deep but ever present!
I do not know from whence it comes.
It is the forefather of the gods.

FIVE

Heaven and earth are impartial;
They see the ten thousand things as straw dogs.
The wise are impartial;
They see the people as straw dogs.

The space between heaven and earth is like a bellows.
The shape changes but not the form;
The more it moves, the more it yields.
More words count less.
Hold fast to the center.

SIX

The valley spirit never dies;
It is the woman, primal mother.
Her gateway is the root of heaven and earth.
It is like a veil barely seen.
Use it; it will never fail.

SEVEN

Heaven and earth last forever.
Why do heaven and earth last forever?
They are unborn,
So ever living.
The sage stays behind, thus he is ahead.
He is detached, thus at one with all.
Through selfless action, he attains fulfillment.

EIGHT

The highest good is like water.
Water gives life to the ten thousand things and does not strive.
It flows in places men reject and so is like the Tao.

In dwelling, be close to the land.
In meditation, go deep in the heart.
In dealing with others, be gentle and kind.
In speech, be true.
In ruling, be just.
In daily life, be competent.
In action, be aware of the time and the season.

No fight: No blame.

NINE

Better stop short than fill to the brim.
Oversharpen the blade, and the edge will soon blunt.
Amass a store of gold and jade, and no one can protect it.
Claim wealth and titles, and disaster will follow.
Retire when the work is done.
This is the way of heaven.

TEN

Carrying body and soul and embracing the one,
Can you avoid separation?
Attending fully and becoming supple,
Can you be as a newborn babe?
Washing and cleansing the primal vision,
Can you be without stain?
Loving all men and ruling the country,
Can you be without cleverness?
Opening and closing the gates of heaven,
Can you play the role of woman?
Understanding and being open to all things,
Are you able to do nothing?
Giving birth and nourishing,
Bearing yet not possessing,
Working yet not taking credit,
Leading yet not dominating,
This is the Primal Virtue.

ELEVEN

Thirty spokes share the wheel's hub;
It is the center hole that makes it useful.
Shape clay into a vessel;
It is the space within that makes it useful.
Cut doors and windows for a room;
It is the holes which make it useful.
Therefore benefit comes from what is there;
Usefulness from what is not there.

TWELVE

The five colors blind the eye.
The five tones deafen the ear.
The five flavors dull the taste.
Racing and hunting madden the mind.
Precious things lead one astray.

Therefore the sage is guided by what he feels and not
    by what he sees.
He lets go of that and chooses this.

THIRTEEN

Accept disgrace willingly.
Accept misfortune as the human condition.

What do you mean by "Accept disgrace willingly"?
Accept being unimportant.
Do not be concerned with loss or gain.
This is called "accepting disgrace willingly."

What do you mean by "Accept misfortune as the human
  condition"?
Misfortune comes from having a body.
Without a body, how could there be misfortune?

Surrender yourself humbly; then you can be trusted to care
  for all things.
Love the world as your own self; then you can truly care for
  all things.

FOURTEEN

Look, it cannot be seen — it is beyond form.
Listen, it cannot be heard — it is beyond sound.
Grasp, it cannot be held — it is intangible.
These three are indefinable;
Therefore they are joined in one.

From above it is not bright;
From below it is not dark:
An unbroken thread beyond description.
It returns to nothingness.
The form of the formless,
The image of the imageless,
It is called indefinable and beyond imagination.

Stand before it and there is no beginning.
Follow it and there is no end.
Stay with the ancient Tao,
Move with the present.

Knowing the ancient beginning is the essence of Tao.

FIFTEEN

The ancient masters were subtle, mysterious, profound,
    responsive.
The depth of their knowledge is unfathomable.
Because it is unfathomable,
All we can do is describe their appearance.
Watchful, like men crossing a winter stream.
Alert, like men aware of danger.
Courteous, like visiting guests.
Yielding, like ice about to melt.
Simple, like uncarved blocks of wood.
Hollow, like caves.
Opaque, like muddy pools.

Who can wait quietly while the mud settles?
Who can remain still until the moment of action?
Observers of the Tao do not seek fulfillment.
Not seeking fulfillment, they are not swayed by desire for
    change.

SIXTEEN

Empty yourself of everything.
Let the mind become still.
The ten thousand things rise and fall while the Self watches
    their return.
They grow and flourish and then return to the source.
Returning to the source is stillness, which is the way of nature.
The way of nature is unchanging.
Knowing constancy is insight.
Not knowing constancy leads to disaster.
Knowing constancy, the mind is open.
With an open mind, you will be openhearted.
Being openhearted, you will act royally.
Being royal, you will attain the divine.
Being divine, you will be at one with the Tao.
Being at one with the Tao is eternal.
And though the body dies, the Tao will never pass away.

SEVENTEEN

The very highest is barely known.
Then comes that which people know and love,
Then that which is feared,
Then that which is despised.

Who does not trust enough will not be trusted.

When actions are performed
Without unnecessary speech,
People say, "We did it!"

EIGHTEEN

When the great Tao is forgotten,
Kindness and morality arise.
When wisdom and intelligence are born,
The great pretence begins.

When there is no peace within the family,
Filial piety and devotion arise.
When the country is confused and in chaos,
Loyal ministers appear.

NINETEEN

Give up sainthood, renounce wisdom,
And it will be a hundred times better for everyone.

Give up kindness, renounce morality,
And men will rediscover filial piety and love.

Give up ingenuity, renounce profit,
And bandits and thieves will disappear.

These three are outward forms alone; they are not sufficient
    in themselves.
It is more important
To see the simplicity,
To realize one's true nature,
To cast off selfishness
And temper desire.

TWENTY

Give up learning, and put an end to your troubles.

Is there a difference between yes and no?
Is there a difference between good and evil?
Must I fear what others fear? What nonsense!
Other people are contented, enjoying the sacrificial feast of
    the ox.
In spring some go to the park, and climb the terrace,
But I alone am drifting, not knowing where I am.
Like a newborn babe before it learns to smile,
I am alone, without a place to go.

Others have more than they need, but I alone have nothing.
I am a fool. Oh, yes! I am confused.
Others are clear and bright,
But I alone am dim and weak.
Others are sharp and clever,
But I alone am dull and stupid.
Oh, I drift like the waves of the sea,
Without direction, like the restless wind.

Everyone else is busy,
But I alone am aimless and depressed.
I am different.
I am nourished by the great mother.

TWENTY-ONE

The greatest Virtue is to follow Tao and Tao alone.
The Tao is elusive and intangible.
Oh, it is intangible and elusive, and yet within is image.
Oh, it is elusive and intangible, and yet within is form.
Oh, it is dim and dark, and yet within is essence.
This essence is very real, and therein lies faith.
From the very beginning until now its name has never been
    forgotten.
Thus I perceive the creation.
How do I know the ways of creation?
Because of this.

TWENTY-TWO

Yield and overcome;
Bend and be straight;
Empty and be full;
Wear out and be new;
Have little and gain;
Have much and be confused.

Therefore the wise embrace the one
And set an example to all.
Not putting on a display,
They shine forth.
Not justifying themselves,
They are distinguished.
Not boasting,
They receive recognition.
Not bragging,
They never falter.
They do not quarrel,
So no one quarrels with them.
Therefore the ancients say, "Yield and overcome."
Is that an empty saying?
Be really whole,
And all things will come to you.

TWENTY-THREE

To talk little is natural.
High winds do not last all morning.
Heavy rain does not last all day.
Why is this? Heaven and earth!
If heaven and earth cannot make things eternal,
How is it possible for man?

He who follows the Tao
Is at one with the Tao.
He who is virtuous
Experiences Virtue.
He who loses the way
Is lost.
When you are at one with the Tao,
The Tao welcomes you.
When you are at one with Virtue,
The Virtue is always there.
When you are at one with loss,
The loss is experienced willingly.

He who does not trust enough
Will not be trusted.

TWENTY-FOUR

He who stands on tiptoe is not steady.
He who strides cannot maintain the pace.
He who makes a show is not enlightened.
He who is self-righteous is not respected.
He who boasts achieves nothing.
He who brags will not endure.
According to followers of the Tao, "These are extra food
    and unnecessary luggage."
They do not bring happiness.
Therefore followers of the Tao avoid them.

TWENTY-FIVE

Something mysteriously formed,
Born before heaven and earth.
In the silence and the void,
Standing alone and unchanging,
Ever present and in motion.
Perhaps it is the mother of ten thousand things.
I do not know its name
Call it Tao.
For lack of a better word, I call it great.

Being great, it flows.
It flows far away.
Having gone far, it returns.

Therefore, "Tao is great;
Heaven is great;
Earth is great;
The king is also great."
These are the four great powers of the universe,
And the king is one of them.

Man follows the earth.
Earth follows heaven.
Heaven follows the Tao.
Tao follows what is natural.

TWENTY-SIX

The heavy is the root of the light;
The still is the master of unrest.

Therefore the sage, traveling all day,
Does not lose sight of his baggage.
Though there are beautiful things to be seen,
He remains unattached and calm.

Why should the lord of ten thousand chariots
    act lightly in public?
To be light is to lose one's root.
To be restless is to lose one's control.

TWENTY-SEVEN

A good walker leaves no tracks;
A good speaker makes no slips;
A good reckoner needs no tally.
A good door needs no lock,
Yet no one can open it.
Good binding requires no knots,
Yet no one can loosen it.

Therefore the sage takes care of all men
And abandons no one.
He takes care of all things
And abandons nothing.

This is called "following the light."

What is a good man?
A teacher of a bad man.
What is a bad man?
A good man's charge.
If the teacher is not respected,
And the student not cared for,
Confusion will arise, however clever one is.
This is the crux of mystery.

TWENTY-EIGHT

Know the strength of man,
But keep a woman's care!
Be the stream of the universe!
Being the stream of the universe,
Ever true and unswerving,
Become as a little child once more.

Know the white,
But keep the black!
Be an example to the world!
Being an example to the world,
Ever true and unwavering,
Return to the infinite.

Know honor,
Yet keep humility.
Be the valley of the universe!
Being the valley of the universe,
Ever true and resourceful,
Return to the state of the uncarved block.

When the block is carved, it becomes useful.
When the sage uses it, he becomes the ruler.
Thus, "A great tailor cuts little."

TWENTY-NINE

Do you think you can take over the universe and improve it?
I do not believe it can be done.

The universe is sacred.
You cannot improve it.
If you try to change it, you will ruin it.
If you try to hold it, you will lose it.

So sometimes things are ahead and sometimes they are
   behind;
Sometimes breathing is hard, sometimes it comes easily;
Sometimes there is strength and sometimes weakness;
Sometimes one is up and sometimes down.

Therefore the sage avoids extremes, excesses, and complacency.

THIRTY

Whenever you advise a ruler in the way of Tao,
Counsel him not to use force to conquer the universe.
For this would only cause resistance.
Thorn bushes spring up wherever the army has passed.
Lean years follow in the wake of a great war.
Just do what needs to be done.
Never take advantage of power.

Achieve results,
But never glory in them.
Achieve results,
But never boast.
Achieve results,
But never be proud.
Achieve results,
Because this is the natural way.
Achieve results,
But not through violence.

Force is followed by loss of strength.
This is not the way of Tao.
That which goes against the Tao comes to an early end.

THIRTY-ONE

Good weapons are instruments of fear; all creatures hate them.
Therefore followers of Tao never use them.
The wise man prefers the left.
The man of war prefers the right.

Weapons are instruments of fear; they are not a wise man's
    tools.
He uses them only when he has no choice.
Peace and quiet are dear to his heart,
And victory no cause for rejoicing.
If you rejoice in victory, then you delight in killing;
If you delight in killing, you cannot fulfill yourself.

On happy occasions precedence is given to the left,
On sad occasions to the right.
In the army the general stands on the left,
The commander-in-chief on the right.
This means that war is conducted like a funeral.
When many people are being killed,
They should be mourned in heartfelt sorrow.
That is why a victory must be observed like a funeral.

THIRTY-TWO

The Tao is forever undefined.
Small though it is in the unformed state, it cannot
    be grasped.
If kings and lords could harness it,
The ten thousand things would naturally obey.
Heaven and earth would come together
And gentle rain fall.
Men would need no more instruction and all things
    would take their course.

Once the whole is divided, the parts need names.
There are already enough names.
One must know when to stop.
Knowing when to stop averts trouble.
Tao in the world is like a river flowing home to the sea.

THIRTY-THREE

Knowing others is wisdom;
Knowing the self is enlightenment.
Mastering others requires force;
Mastering the self needs strength.

He who knows he has enough is rich.
Perseverance is a sign of willpower.
He who stays where he is endures.
To die but not to perish is to be eternally present.

THIRTY-FOUR

The great Tao flows everywhere, both to the left
    and to the right.
The ten thousand things depend upon it; it holds
    nothing back.
It fulfills its purpose silently and makes no claim.

It nourishes the ten thousand things,
And yet is not their lord.
It has no aim; it is very small.

The ten thousand things return to it,
Yet it is not their lord.
It is very great.

It does not show greatness,
And is therefore truly great.

THIRTY-FIVE

All men will come to him who keeps to the one,
For there lie rest and happiness and peace.

Passersby may stop for music and good food,
But a description of the Tao
Seems without substance or flavor.
It cannot be seen, it cannot be heard,
And yet it cannot be exhausted.

THIRTY-SIX

That which shrinks
Must first expand.
That which fails
Must first be strong.
That which is cast down
Must first be raised.
Before receiving
There must be giving.

This is called perception of the nature of things.
Soft and weak overcome hard and strong.

Fish cannot leave deep waters,
And a country's weapons should not be displayed.

THIRTY-SEVEN

Tao abides in non-action,
Yet nothing is left undone.
If kings and lords observed this,
The ten thousand things would develop naturally.
If they still desired to act,
They would return to the simplicity of formless substance.
Without form there is no desire.
Without desire there is tranquillity.
And in this way all things would be at peace.

THIRTY-EIGHT

A truly good man is not aware of his goodness,
And is therefore good.
A foolish man tries to be good,
And is therefore not good.

A truly good man does nothing,
Yet leaves nothing undone.
A foolish man is always doing,
Yet much remains to be done.

When a truly kind man does something, he leaves
    nothing undone.
When a just man does something, he leaves a great deal
    to be done.
When a disciplinarian does something and no one responds,
He rolls up his sleeves in an attempt to enforce order.

Therefore when Tao is lost, there is goodness.
When goodness is lost, there is kindness.
When kindness is lost, there is justice.
When justice is lost, there is ritual.
Now ritual is the husk of faith and loyalty, the beginning
    of confusion.
Knowledge of the future is only a flowery trapping of Tao.
It is the beginning of folly.

Therefore the truly great man dwells on what is real and
    not what is on the surface,
On the fruit and not the flower.
Therefore accept the one and reject the other.

THIRTY-NINE

These things from ancient times arise from one:
The sky is whole and clear.
The earth is whole and firm.
The spirit is whole and strong.
The valley is whole and full.
The ten thousand things are whole and alive.
Kings and lords are whole, and the country is upright.
All these are in virtue of wholeness.

The clarity of the sky prevents its falling.
The firmness of the earth prevents its splitting.
The strength of the spirit prevents its being used up.
The fullness of the valley prevents its running dry.
The growth of the ten thousand things prevents
    their dying out.
The leadership of kings and lords prevents the downfall
    of the country.

Therefore the humble is the root of the noble.
The low is the foundation of the high.
Princes and lords consider themselves
    "orphaned," "widowed," and "worthless."
Do they not depend on being humble?

Too much success is not an advantage.
Do not tinkle like jade
Or clatter like stone chimes.

FORTY

Returning is the motion of the Tao.
Yielding is the way of the Tao.
The ten thousand things are born of being.
Being is born of not being.

FORTY-ONE

The wise student hears of the Tao and practices it diligently.
The average student hears of the Tao and gives it thought
    now and again.
The foolish student hears of the Tao and laughs aloud.
If there were no laughter, the Tao would not be what it is.

Hence it is said:
The bright path seems dim;
Going forward seems like retreat;
The easy way seems hard;
The highest Virtue seems empty;
Great purity seems sullied;
A wealth of Virtue seems inadequate;
The strength of Virtue seems frail;
Real Virtue seems unreal;
The perfect square has no corners;
Great talents ripen late;
The highest notes are hard to hear;
The greatest form has no shape.
The Tao is hidden and without name.
The Tao alone nourishes and brings everything to fulfillment.

FORTY-TWO

The Tao begot one.
One begot two.
Two begot three.
And three begot the ten thousand things.

The ten thousand things carry yin and embrace yang.
They achieve harmony by combining these forces.

Men hate to be "orphaned," "widowed," or "worthless,"
But this is how kings and lords describe themselves.

For one gains by losing
And loses by gaining.

What others teach, I also teach; that is:
"A violent man will die a violent death!"
This will be the essence of my teaching.

FORTY-THREE

The softest thing in the universe
Overcomes the hardest thing in the universe.
That without substance can enter where there is no room.
Hence I know the value of non-action.

Teaching without words and work without doing
Are understood by very few.

FORTY-FOUR

Fame or self: Which matters more?
Self or wealth: Which is more precious?
Gain or loss: Which is more painful?

He who is attached to things will suffer much.
He who saves will suffer heavy loss.
A contented man is never disappointed.
He who knows when to stop does not find himself in trouble.
He will stay forever safe.

FORTY-FIVE

Great accomplishment seems imperfect,
Yet it does not outlive its usefulness.
Great fullness seems empty,
Yet it cannot be exhausted.

Great straightness seems twisted.
Great intelligence seems stupid.
Great eloquence seems awkward.

Movement overcomes cold.
Stillness overcomes heat.
Stillness and tranquillity set things in order in the universe.

FORTY-SIX

When the Tao is present in the universe,
The horses haul manure.
When the Tao is absent from the universe,
War horses are bred outside the city.

There is no greater sin than desire,
No greater curse than discontent,
No greater misfortune than wanting something for oneself.
Therefore he who knows that enough is enough will always
    have enough.

FORTY-SEVEN

Without going outside, you may know the whole world.
Without looking through the window, you may see the ways
    of heaven.
The farther you go, the less you know.

Thus the sage knows without traveling;
He sees without looking;
He works without doing.

FORTY-EIGHT

In the pursuit of learning, every day something is acquired.
In the pursuit of Tao, every day something is dropped.

Less and less is done
Until non-action is achieved.
When nothing is done, nothing is left undone.

The world is ruled by letting things take their course.
It cannot be ruled by interfering.

FORTY-NINE

The sage has no mind of his own.
He is aware of the needs of others.

I am good to people who are good.
I am also good to people who are not good.
Because Virtue is goodness.
I have faith in people who are faithful.
I also have faith in people who are not faithful.
Because Virtue is faithfulness.

The sage is shy and humble — to the world
     he seems confusing.
Others look to him and listen.
He behaves like a little child.

FIFTY

Between birth and death,
Three in ten are followers of life,
Three in ten are followers of death,
And men just passing from birth to death
    also number three in ten.
Why is this so?
Because they live their lives on the gross level.

He who knows how to live can walk abroad
Without fear of rhinoceros or tiger.
He will not be wounded in battle.
For in him rhinoceroses can find no place to
    thrust their horn,
Tigers no place to use their claws,
And weapons no place to pierce.
Why is this so?
Because he has no place for death to enter.

FIFTY-ONE

All things arise from Tao.
They are nourished by Virtue.
They are formed from matter.
They are shaped by environment.
Thus the ten thousand things all respect Tao and
    honor Virtue.
Respect of Tao and honor of Virtue are not demanded,
But they are in the nature of things.

Therefore all things arise from Tao.
By Virtue they are nourished,
Developed, cared for,
Sheltered, comforted,
Grown, and protected.
Creating without claiming,
Doing without taking credit,
Guiding without interfering,
This is Primal Virtue.

FIFTY-TWO

The beginning of the universe
Is the mother of all things.
Knowing the mother, one also knows the sons.
Knowing the sons, yet remaining in touch with the mother,
Brings freedom from the fear of death.

Keep your mouth shut,
Guard the senses,
And life is ever full.
Open your mouth,
Always be busy,
And life is beyond hope.

Seeing the small is insight;
Yielding to force is strength.
Using the outer light, return to insight,
And in this way be saved from harm.
This is learning constancy.

FIFTY-THREE

If I have even just a little sense,
I will walk on the main road and my only fear will be
    of straying from it.
Keeping to the main road is easy,
But people love to be sidetracked.

When the court is arrayed in splendor,
The fields are full of weeds,
And the granaries are bare.
Some wear gorgeous clothes,
Carry sharp swords,
And indulge themselves with food and drink;
They have more possessions than they can use.
They are robber barons.
This is certainly not the way of Tao.

FIFTY-FOUR

What is firmly established cannot be uprooted.
What is firmly grasped cannot slip away.
It will be honored from generation to generation.

Cultivate Virtue in your self,
And Virtue will be real.
Cultivate it in the family,
And Virtue will abound.
Cultivate it in the village,
And Virtue will grow.
Cultivate it in the nation,
And Virtue will be abundant.
Cultivate it in the universe,
And Virtue will be everywhere.

Therefore look at the body as body;
Look at the family as family;
Look at the village as village;
Look at the nation as nation;
Look at the universe as universe.

How do I know the universe is like this?
By looking!

FIFTY-FIVE

He who is filled with Virtue is like a newborn child.
Wasps and serpents will not sting him;
Wild beasts will not pounce upon him;
He will not be attacked by birds of prey.
His bones are soft, his muscles weak,
But his grip is firm.
He has not experienced the union of man and woman,
    but is whole.
His manhood is strong.
He screams all day without becoming hoarse.
This is perfect harmony.

Knowing harmony is constancy.
Knowing constancy is enlightenment.

It is not wise to rush about.
Controlling the breath causes strain.
If too much energy is used, exhaustion follows.
This is not the way of Tao.
Whatever is contrary to Tao will not last long.

FIFTY-SIX

Those who know do not talk.
Those who talk do not know.

Keep your mouth closed.
Guard your senses.
Temper your sharpness.
Simplify your problems.
Mask your brightness.
Be at one with the dust of the earth.
This is primal union.

He who has achieved this state
Is unconcerned with friends and enemies,
With good and harm, with honor and disgrace.
This therefore is the highest state of man.

FIFTY-SEVEN

Rule a nation with justice.
Wage war with surprise moves.
Become master of the universe without striving.
How do I know that this is so?
Because of this!

The more laws and restrictions there are,
The poorer people become.
The sharper men's weapons,
The more trouble in the land.
The more ingenious and clever men are,
The more strange things happen.
The more rules and regulations,
The more thieves and robbers.

Therefore the sage says:
   I take no action and people are reformed.
   I enjoy peace and people become honest.
   I do nothing and people become rich.
   I have no desires and people return to the good
      and simple life.

FIFTY-EIGHT

When the country is ruled with a light hand
The people are simple.
When the country is ruled with severity,
The people are cunning.

Happiness is rooted in misery.
Misery lurks beneath happiness.
Who knows what the future holds?
There is no honesty.
Honesty becomes dishonest.
Goodness becomes witchcraft.
Man's bewitchment lasts for a long time.

Therefore the sage is sharp but not cutting,
Pointed but not piercing,
Straightforward but not unrestrained,
Brilliant but not blinding.

FIFTY-NINE

In caring for others and serving heaven,
There is nothing like using restraint.
Restraint begins with giving up one's own ideas.
This depends on Virtue gathered in the past.
If there is a good store of Virtue, then nothing is impossible.
If nothing is impossible, then there are no limits.
If a man knows no limits, then he is fit to be a ruler.
The mother principle of ruling holds good for a long time.
This is called having deep roots and a firm foundation,
The Tao of long life and eternal vision.

SIXTY

Ruling the country is like cooking a small fish.
Approach the universe with Tao,
And evil will have no power.
Not that evil is not powerful,
But its power will not be used to harm others.
Not only will it do no harm to others,
But the sage himself will also be protected.
They do not hurt each other,
And the Virtue in each one refreshes both.

SIXTY-ONE

A great country is like low land.
It is the meeting ground of the universe,
The mother of the universe.

The female overcomes the male with stillness,
Lying low in stillness.

Therefore if a great country gives way to a smaller country,
It will conquer the smaller country.
And if a small country submits to a great country,
It can conquer the great country.
Therefore those who would conquer must yield,
And those who conquer do so because they yield.

A great nation needs more people;
A small country needs to serve.
Each gets what it wants.
It is fitting for a great nation to yield.

SIXTY-TWO

Tao is the source of the ten thousand things.
It is the treasure of the good man, and the refuge of the bad.
Sweet words can buy honor;
Good deeds can gain respect.
If a man is bad, do not abandon him.
Therefore on the day the emperor is crowned,
Or the three officers of state installed,
Do not send a gift of jade and a team of four horses,
But remain still and offer the Tao.
Why does everyone like the Tao so much at first?
Isn't it because you find what you seek and are forgiven
    when you sin?
Therefore this is the greatest treasure of the universe.

SIXTY-THREE

Practice non-action.
Work without doing.
Taste the tasteless.
Magnify the small, increase the few.
Reward bitterness with care.

See simplicity in the complicated.
Achieve greatness in little things.

In the universe the difficult things are done
    as if they are easy.
In the universe great acts are made up of small deeds.
The sage does not attempt anything very big,
And thus achieves greatness.

Easy promises make for little trust.
Taking things lightly results in great difficulty.
Because the sage always confronts difficulties,
He never experiences them.

SIXTY-FOUR

Peace is easily maintained;
Trouble is easily overcome before it starts.
The brittle is easily shattered;
The small is easily scattered.

Deal with it before it happens.
Set things in order before there is confusion.

A tree as great as a man's embrace springs from a small shoot;
A terrace nine stories high begins with a pile of earth;
A journey of a thousand miles starts under one's feet.

He who acts defeats his own purpose;
He who grasps loses.
The sage does not act, and so is not defeated.
He does not grasp and therefore does not lose.

People usually fail when they are on the verge of success.
So give as much care to the end as to the beginning;
Then there will be no failure.

Therefore the sage seeks freedom from desire.
He does not collect precious things.
He learns not to hold on to ideas.
He brings men back to what they have lost.
He helps the ten thousand things find their own nature,
But refrains from action.

SIXTY-FIVE

In the beginning those who knew the Tao
    did not try to enlighten others,
But kept it hidden.
Why is it so hard to rule?
Because people are so clever.
Rulers who try to use cleverness
Cheat the country.
Those who rule without cleverness
Are a blessing to the land.
These are the two alternatives.
Understanding these is Primal Virtue.
Primal Virtue is deep and far.
It leads all things back
Toward the great oneness.

SIXTY-SIX

Why is the sea king of a hundred streams?
Because it lies below them.
Therefore it is the king of a hundred streams.

If the sage would guide the people, he must serve
    with humility.
If he would lead them, he must follow behind.
In this way when the sage rules, the people
    will not feel oppressed;
When he stands before them, they will not be harmed.
The whole world will support him and will not tire of him.

Because he does not compete,
He does not meet competition.

SIXTY-SEVEN

Everyone under heaven says that my Tao is great
　　and beyond compare.
Because it is great, it seems different.
If it were not different, it would have vanished long ago.

I have three treasures which I hold and keep.
The first is mercy; the second is economy;
The third is daring not to be ahead of others.
From mercy comes courage; from economy comes generosity;
From humility comes leadership.

Nowadays men shun mercy, but try to be brave;
They abandon economy, but try to be generous;
They do not believe in humility, but always try to be first.
This is certain death.

Mercy brings victory in battle and strength in defense.
It is the means by which heaven saves and guards.

SIXTY-EIGHT

A good soldier is not violent.
A good fighter is not angry.
A good winner is not vengeful.
A good employer is humble.
This is known as the Virtue of not striving.
This is known as ability to deal with people.
This since ancient times has been known
    as the ultimate unity with heaven.

SIXTY-NINE

There is a saying among soldiers:
    I dare not make the first move but would rather
        play the guest;
    I dare not advance an inch but would rather
        withdraw a foot.

This is called marching without appearing to move,
Rolling up your sleeves without showing your arm,
Capturing the enemy without attacking,
Being armed without weapons.

There is no greater catastrophe than underestimating
    the enemy.
By underestimating the enemy, I almost lose what I value.

Therefore when the battle is joined,
The underdog will win.

SEVENTY

My words are easy to understand and easy to perform,
Yet no man under heaven knows them or practices them.

My words have ancient beginnings.
My actions are disciplined.
Because men do not understand, they have
     no knowledge of me.

Those that know me are few;
Those that abuse me are honored.
Therefore the sage wears rough clothing and
     holds the jewel in his heart.

SEVENTY-ONE

Knowing ignorance is strength.
Ignoring knowledge is sickness.

If one is sick of sickness, then one is not sick.
The sage is not sick because he is sick of sickness.
Therefore he is not sick.

SEVENTY-TWO

When men lack a sense of awe, there will be disaster.

Do not intrude in their homes.
Do not harass them at work.
If you do not interfere, they will not weary of you.

Therefore the sage knows himself but makes no show,
Has self-respect but is not arrogant.
He lets go of that and chooses this.

SEVENTY-THREE

A brave and passionate man will kill or be killed.
A brave and calm man will always preserve life.
Of these two which is good and which is harmful?
Some things are not favored by heaven. Who knows why?
Even the sage is unsure of this.

The Tao of heaven does not strive, and yet it overcomes.
It does not speak, and yet is answered.
It does not ask, yet is supplied with all its needs.
It seems to have no aim and yet its purpose is fulfilled.

Heaven's net casts wide.
Though its meshes are coarse, nothing slips through.

SEVENTY-FOUR

If men are not afraid to die,
It is of no avail to threaten them with death.

If men live in constant fear of dying,
And if breaking the law means that a man will be killed,
Who will dare to break the law?

There is always an official executioner.
If you try to take his place,
It is like trying to be a master carpenter and cutting wood.
If you try to cut wood like a master carpenter,
    you will only hurt your hand.

SEVENTY-FIVE

Why are the people starving?
Because the rulers eat up the money in taxes.
Therefore the people are starving.

Why are the people rebellious?
Because the rulers interfere too much.
Therefore they are rebellious.

Why do the people think so little of death?
Because the rulers demand too much of life.
Therefore the people take death lightly.

Having little to live on, one knows better than
 to value life too much.

SEVENTY-SIX

A man is born gentle and weak.
At his death he is hard and stiff.
Green plants are tender and filled with sap.
At their death they are withered and dry.

Therefore the stiff and unbending is the disciple of death.
The gentle and yielding is the disciple of life.

Thus an army without flexibility never wins a battle.
A tree that is unbending is easily broken.

The hard and strong will fall.
The soft and weak will overcome.

SEVENTY-SEVEN

The Tao of heaven is like the bending of a bow.
The high is lowered, and the low is raised.
If the string is too long, it is shortened;
If there is not enough, it is made longer.

The Tao of heaven is to take from those who have too much
    and give to those who do not have enough.
Man's way is different.
He takes from those who do not have enough to give to those
    who already have too much.
What man has more than enough and gives it to the world?
Only the man of Tao.

Therefore the sage works without recognition.
He achieves what has to be done without dwelling on it.
He does not try to show his knowledge.

SEVENTY-EIGHT

Under heaven nothing is more soft and yielding than water.
Yet for attacking the solid and strong, nothing is better;
It has no equal.
The weak can overcome the strong;
The supple can overcome the stiff.
Under heaven everyone knows this,
Yet no one puts it into practice.
Therefore the sage says:
  He who takes upon himself the humiliation of the people
     is fit to rule them.
  He who takes upon himself the country's disasters
     deserves to be king of the universe.
The truth often sounds paradoxical.

SEVENTY-NINE

After a bitter quarrel, some resentment must remain.
What can one do about it?
Therefore the sage keeps his half of the bargain
But does not exact his due.
A man of Virtue performs his part,
But a man without Virtue requires others to fulfill
    their obligations.
The Tao of heaven is impartial.
It stays with good men all the time.

EIGHTY

A small country has fewer people.
Though there are machines that can work ten to a hundred
     times faster than man, they are not needed.
The people take death seriously and do not travel far.
Though they have boats and carriages, no one uses them.
Though they have armor and weapons, no one displays them.
Men return to the knotting of rope in place of writing.
Their food is plain and good, their clothes fine but simple,
     their homes secure;
They are happy in their ways.
Though they live within sight of their neighbors,
And crowing cocks and barking dogs are heard across the way,
Yet they leave each other in peace while they grow old and die.

EIGHTY-ONE

Truthful words are not beautiful.
Beautiful words are not truthful.
Good men do not argue.
Those who argue are not good.
Those who know are not learned.
The learned do not know.

The sage never tries to store things up.
The more he does for others, the more he has.
The more he gives to others, the greater his abundance.
The Tao of heaven is pointed but does no harm.
The Tao of the sage is work without effort.

NOTES, COMMENTS, AND ECHOES

It is not my intention here to present historical material or extensive interpretations of the text. Several good academic commentaries are suggested in the selected bibliography. I offer the following only as my own thoughts based on examination of other translations and on the study of many other spiritual philosophies and traditions.

ONE

This famous opening might also be rendered as "The way that can be explained is not the eternal Way" or "The path that is well-marked is not the eternal Path." Although the true Way or Path has always existed in eternity and rigorously conforms to precise laws, it must always be discovered for oneself. It is always new. One must always struggle to free oneself from the spell of thoughts and images that are at best reflective only of what has been experienced in the past. The "ordinary," isolated

85

intellect is not the agent through which the living, present moment can be experienced. This ordinary mind is prey to countless suggestions and associations that can impede the experience of reality, and among the most seductive of these suggestions are those that have spiritual or religious content. "The Truth," said Krishnamurti, "is a pathless land." The real guide, therefore, does not only give the pupil the truth but offers conditions that help the pupil discover the truth for himself.

Some comment on the meaning of *desire* may be of help here. In this chapter no negative judgment is applied to *desiring*, although other translators, such as Paul Carus, have thought otherwise. Carus has "But he who is by desire bound/Sees the mere shell of things around." The present translation may be taken to suggest mainly that through the desires one is drawn toward the manifestations of the ultimate source. These manifestations are "the ten thousand things" and have their own reality, in other words, real effects of the real cause. Trouble begins only when one mistakes the effects for the cause. The main point to be noted here is that the word *desire* can refer to something morally neutral within us or, in other contexts, to the main abnormality and distortion of our nature. In the latter case a more accurate word would be *addiction* or *craving*, which is what a desire becomes when we allow it to absorb the finer energies of our psyche. Craving is a desire that devours us. But desires pure and simple are not to be killed or suppressed; they are an aspect of our human nature, which enter importantly into the process of inner transformation at a certain stage of the way. Confusion between these two meanings has resulted in a great misunderstanding of many spiritual, religious, and philosophical teachings through the ages. In the present translation the context usually makes it quite clear which sense of *desire* Lao Tsu intended.

TWO

The world of manifestation is a world in which all phenomena are the result of the interplay of two opposing forces. It is wisdom to realize that everything one can see in this world has its opposite. Every force evokes and depends upon a counterforce. Distortion and illusion come from not understanding this, from affirming the "good," for example, and ignoring or naively seeking to destroy that which opposes the good. The wise understand all of life amid the ten thousand things as basically a play of forces. Moral teachings that attempt to break the complementary relation of "good" and "evil" are doomed to failure, and breed violence to others and to oneself. This teaching is an essential aspect of the doctrine that has, in the Western world, often been condemned as heretical or dangerous. In any case it is always a difficult, hidden, and subtle doctrine, easily misunderstood as justifying self-indulgence and even cruelty. Nietzsche's famous "beyond good and evil" echoes this doctrine, and the crimes that have been committed under this banner are ample testimony to the need to understand it only in the context of a complete spiritual teaching. In Judaism and Islam this idea often forms part of the "esoteric" path, reserved for those who have passed through the moral discipline and training of the "exoteric" or orthodox tradition. Every complete religious tradition comprises these different levels of understanding and practice.

THREE

The wise rule by freeing people, and themselves, from attachment to desires; by helping to strengthen the essential in human nature, "stuffing bellies" and "strengthening bones"; and by reducing the lopsided dependence on acquired mental knowledge and artificially induced desires. According to the twentieth-century spiritual teacher G. I. Gurdjieff, a human being is made up of essence and personality. "Essence" is what is one's own, what one is born with; "personality" is acquired as the result of education and social conditioning. Both are necessary to human life, but each must develop in proper relation to the other.

FIVE

"Straw dogs," as Wing-Tsit Chan and others point out, "were used for sacrifices in ancient China. After they had been used, they were thrown away and there was no more sentimental attachment to them."[1] These lines suggest the universal scale against which the wise measure human values. Man has a cosmic destiny, whereas most of what we call morality concerns relative and ephemeral social values, often having to do mainly with what is good or bad only for the individual person or group. The impartiality of the wise refers to the universal context within which they understand the meaning of human life and its possibilities. The highest forces can care for us only to the extent

---

[1] Wing-Tsit Chan, *The Way of Lao Tzu* (Indianapolis and New York: Bobbs-Merrill Co., 1963), 108.

that we allow them into our own being. In *The Guide for the Perplexed,* the great twelfth-century Jewish spiritual philosopher Moses Maimonides states that God's providence can act in human life only to the extent that man's intellect is in actual contact with God. Otherwise, human beings are like "cattle" and subject to accidents of every kind. This perspective was never completely incorporated into the mainstream of orthodox Judaism.

EIGHT

Water is one of Lao Tsu's principal symbols for the Tao, along with the infant, the female, the valley, and the uncarved block. He who lives the Tao acts in his life and dealings as water acts in nature. Water does not resist, yet it conquers all; it is tasteless — suggesting the invisibility of the Tao — yet life-giving. It moves through all that lives and in movement remains clear and pure. It is supple, flexible, and humble; it does not compete; it flows naturally to the lowest places. All things arise from water and return to water. What better image for what Lao Tsu means by *non-being* and *non-acting*?

No fight: No blame. This line tersely expresses the idea that he who does not seek to impose his own will is beyond reproach.

TEN

More than in most versions, the present translation of this chapter carries a hint of the challenge to live fully in the world while maintaining contact with the source — that is, to be man as a two-natured being, embracing the two aspects of reality simultaneously. In the *Bhagavad Gita*, Krishna commands the warrior Arjuna to act strongly in the world but without attachment to the results of action. Consider this also as a possible reading of Christ's dictum "Render unto Caesar that which is Caesar's and unto God that which is God's" (Mark 12:17).

TWELVE

Therefore, the sage is guided by what he feels and not by what he sees. Wing-Tsit Chan, Arthur Waley, Lin Yutang, and most other translators have rendered this line with the word *belly:* "The sage provides for the belly and not for the eye" (Lin Yutang). This usage obviously expresses the same idea as chapter 3, where *belly* refers to the essence, what may be felt and sensed as one's own nature, as opposed to what is seen externally and acquired from outside. The lopsided emphasis on the acquired personality disharmonizes the two-natured being of man. The racing thoughts of the "monkey-mind" experienced in meditation may be understood in this context. In Buddhism this condition of mental agitation is an important aspect of what is called the *samsaric,* or deluded mind.

THIRTEEN

Misfortune comes from having a body: Lin Yutang and Richard
Wilhelm do not take the word *body* literally but rather translate
it as "self" and "persona" respectively. Stephen Mitchell's
version shares the view that this line refers to believing in the
reality of the ego or social self. No doubt there is considerable
truth in such readings, but the present translation may be
pointing us to something even more fundamental — namely, that
the illusion of the ego may itself be rooted in our wrong
relationship to the organic reality of the physical body. Lao Tsu's
teachings about nature obviously preclude our imagining that he
considers the body evil. Perhaps the best echo of the meaning
here is to be found in the Tibetan Buddhist text *The Life of
Milarepa,* in which after his first awesome labors of meditation,
Milarepa tells his teacher: "This body is the blessed vessel for
those fortunate beings who wish for freedom, but it also leads
sinners into the lower realms."[2] Consider also the writings of the
Orthodox Christian Fathers, such as Gregory Palamas. There are
no writings in any tradition that more strongly warn us about the
powers of the body, yet in the midst of all these warnings, we find
St. Gregory saying: "You see, brother, that not only spiritual, but
general human reasoning shows the need to recognize it as
imperative that those who wish to belong to themselves, and to
be truly monks in their inner man, should lead the mind inside
the body and hold it there."[3]

[2] Lobsang P. Lhalungpa, *The Life of Milarepa* (Boulder, Colorado: Prajna Press,
1982), 77.
[3] Gregory Palamas, in E. Kadloubovsky and G. E. H. Palmer, *Early Fathers from
the Philokalia* (London: Faber & Faber, 1954), 405.

SEVENTEEN

This chapter is about different qualities of leadership. In all human undertakings, and especially along the way to self-knowledge, great leadership does not call attention to itself. The guide creates conditions and steers just enough to allow people to search for and experience the truth for themselves. A lesser leader inspires loyalty and affection, but if the pupil does not find his or her own free search, this loyalty will turn negative and become fear and resentment. It would be rewarding to study the fate of spiritual communities, of the present as well as the past, in the light of this chapter. The great master shows trust by the quality of attention he gives the pupil and the respect he shows solely for the pupil's inner work. The story is told of the young Swami Vivekananda, who asked his teacher, Sri Ramakrishna, why he bowed to such an unworthy person as he knew himself to be. Sri Ramakrishna, it is said, replied forcefully: "I am not bowing to *you*! *You* are nothing! I bow to the *atman*, the divine self in you."

EIGHTEEN, NINETEEN, AND TWENTY

These chapters affirm the primacy of being at one with the Tao, rather than thinking about it as an ideal. Lao Tsu warns us that concepts of virtue, ideals of wisdom and morality, and all the precepts that are intended to lead us toward the good all too easily make us forget the main thing, which is to open within ourselves to that radiant energy whose action upon us will conform our lives to the Tao. Consider St. Augustine's "Love

God, and do what you will," and the spontaneous arising of compassion *(karuna)* along the way of the bodhisattva in Mahayana Buddhism. "Morality" is often only the imposition of one part of ourselves (the mind) upon the other parts, which remain, as it were, unconvinced and fundamentally untouched. This does not mean that the seeker of the Way foolishly abandons moral rules, but that at a certain point he sees that external morality without internal morality can be a kind of tyranny over others and over the living forces within oneself. And the *way* toward this inner morality may seem startlingly or even shockingly opposed to "morality." For example, *Give up sainthood, renounce wisdom.* Again, it must be kept in mind that blindly going against conventional morality is as fruitless as blindly obeying convention.

TWENTY-ONE

Because of this: Commentators and translators differ as to the exact meaning of *this.* Is Lao Tsu saying that he knows the ways of creation simply by direct seeing of what he has just described? And should we imagine him pointing to his chest as he says these words? In any case, and speaking more generally, the great metaphysical visions and philosophies of the past are invariably based on what has been directly seen within oneself in the higher states of stillness and meditation. Metaphysics, whether Judeo-Christian, Hindu, Pythagorean, or Taoist, has always been based on experience — the inner experience of man as the mirror of the universe. Such teachings about the cosmos are never mere speculation or based solely on extrapolations from sense observations of the outer world. Here we may rephrase an ancient Hermetic saying: "As above, so within." Only one must learn how to look within. Modern Anglo-American philosophy's tendency to reject metaphysics stems largely from our culture's loss of the art and science of real "seeing."

TWENTY-TWO

Arthur Waley's translation further illuminates the meaning of this chapter:

> To remain whole, be twisted!
> To become straight, let yourself be bent.
> To become full, be hollow.
> Be tattered, that you may be renewed.

TWENTY-THREE

When you are at one with loss,
The loss is experienced willingly.

These lines and what is conjoined with them are perhaps the most puzzling in the whole of the *Tao Te Ching*, so much so that Richard Wilhelm writes, "On the whole, it is probably sensible to give up the passage as hopelessly beyond interpretation."[4] Perhaps the most interesting aspect of the puzzle has to do with the word *loss*. What sort of loss is being spoken of? The present

[4] Richard Wilhelm, *Tao Te Ching* (London and New York: Routledge and Kegan Paul, 1985), 126.

translation says, "He who loses the way/is lost." It does not say, "He who loses the Tao is lost." A great deal hinges on this issue. If it is ordinary loss that is being spoken of (including loss of riches, loss of health, loss of reputation, and so on), then we are being told that the follower of the Tao holds to the Tao in the face of all life circumstances. By contrast, if loss of the Tao is involved, then the matter is much more troubling and interesting. It could mean (as some translators have it) that he who loses the Tao is inwardly so lost that he feels no sense of breaking the contact with the most important thing in life. A more subtle reading could be that he who loses what he *thinks* is the Tao (which is therefore not the Tao that is beyond concepts) voluntarily accepts the sense of loss and is thereby brought back to a deeper movement of return. Yet another reading of this passage, one which I happen to favor and which was offered by the earliest Chinese commentator, Wang Pi, is:

And he who is identified with the abandonment [of Tao] — the abandonment [of Tao] is also happy to abandon him.[5]

In other words, one receives from reality exactly what one seeks from it, "As you sow, so you reap" (Galatians 6:7). The Tao, as the whole of nature, does not violently impose its will. This interpretation has the virtue of corresponding to the opening lines of the chapter.

[5] Ariane Rump with Wing-Tsit Chan, *Commentary on the Lao Tzu by Wang Pi* (Honolulu: University Press of Hawaii, 1979), 71.

TWENTY-FIVE

Tao follows what is natural. This should not be taken to mean that there is a level of reality, called nature, that is distinct from Tao. Tao is spontaneously what it is, through its own nature.

TWENTY-SEVEN

This chapter is important for the light it throws on the way the advanced follower of the Tao, the sage, manifests in the world. I take it to be speaking of the center of gravity of the sage's outward action and the quality of attention he brings to it. To put it simply, the principal intention in the life of the sage is to pass on to others what he has understood of the Way. This, surely, is the highest form of human love, the crux of the mystery in human relationships. Love for one's neighbor here does not mean "liking" the other; it has nothing to do with emotional attraction, nor is it organically or socially conditioned family, sexual, or intellectual love. For the sage, the other is neither "good" nor "bad" — the other is only an individual who is or is not correctly following the Tao. And because all meaning and happiness for humanity depend ultimately on following the Tao, the sage seeks only, and naturally, to arrange the details of his relationship to others to support and further their progress along the way. This is an immensely important issue, within the confines of which lies the whole question of spiritual transmission, communal forms, and the metaphysical basis of ethics.

THIRTY-TWO AND THIRTY-FOUR

Small. In these two chapters and in others (for instance, chapter 52), the word *small* may be taken to mean exceedingly fine, light, invisible, and so on — all these terms referring to that which is the highest and most powerful reality or force in the universe. Such terms invite us to consider as well the quality of awareness that is needed to contact the highest — a very fine, subtle vibration, a consciousness that appears in us under interior conditions of great, vibrant silence. Finally, this "small" awareness may ultimately be understood as the ultimate force itself or, to put it in other terms, mysterious as it may sound: The consciousness of Tao *is* Tao. The highest consciousness is intrinsically consciousness of itself. This self-luminous light expands and descends into the world of the ten thousand things. Compare the use of *small* in the Chandogya Upanishad, III. xiv. 3: "Small as a grain of rice is that Self. . . yet greater than all the worlds." Compare also the mustard seed of the Gospels and the "still, small voice" heard by the prophet Elijah.

THIRTY-THREE

To die but not to perish is to be eternally present: This rendering invites us to think in a fresh way about immortality, what Western religions refer to as the survival of the soul after the death of the body. Something much more dynamic, tangible, and immediately relevant than our usual theological concept of immortality seems to be offered here. What will die? What *must* die? What is presence? — now and here.

THIRTY-EIGHT

Virtue is action that springs spontaneously from the vital center of oneself, not merely action done in conformity to an ideal, however noble, that is held by thought. Compare St. Paul's teaching that Christ came not to destroy the law but to fulfill it — in other words, righteousness is not forcing the body to obey the thought but is rather the appearance of a new principle within ourselves which the body and the mind voluntarily and instantly obey. Compare also Nietzsche's "third metamorphosis of the spirit" in *Thus Spake Zarathustra*, how the spirit became a camel, then a lion, then a child.

FORTY-TWO

From the One the universe is created and at all levels of the world all phenomena are the result of the harmonization of two opposing forces. The wise understand how to live in correspondence with these forces. The foolish identify with one force and are defeated by the counterforce. This is "violence." The wise do not seek to triumph in this way.

FORTY-SEVEN

The human being is a microcosm. By seeing within, one can know the laws of the universe. But, of course, one must understand how to see, how to search within. It is not easy. Compare the *Bhagavad Gita* 4:17: "Know therefore what is work, and also what is wrong work." And 3:27: "All actions take place in time by the interweaving of the forces of Nature; but the man lost in selfish delusion thinks that he himself is the actor."[6]

FORTY-EIGHT

There is nothing to be added. There is nothing missing in ourselves. There are only accretions to be dropped. Compare the Sufi saying:

> When the heart weeps for what it has lost,
> The Spirit laughs for what it has found.

In Christianity this teaching may be discerned in the doctrine that God has already forgiven us; we are already accepted. The human problem is to accept that, deeply. The aim of spiritual work is to become able to receive that love.

FIFTY

Three in ten. . . Paul Carus (and Lin Yutang) offer what seem to me an interesting alternate rendering of these lines:

> There are thirteen avenues of life; there are thirteen avenues of death; on thirteen avenues men that live pass unto the realm of death.
>
> (Carus)

[6] Juan Mascaro, *The Bhagavad Gita* (Harmondsworth, England: Penguin Books, 1962).

The companions (organs) of life are thirteen;
The companions (organs) of death are (also) thirteen.

(Lin Yutang)

He who knows how to live can walk abroad without fear of rhinoceros or tiger. . . What are these rhinoceroses and tigers? Compare Rumi:

A naked man jumps in the river, hornets swarming
above him. The water is the *zikr*, remembering,
There is no reality but God. There is only God.

The hornets are his sexual remembering, this woman,
that woman. Or if a woman, this man, that.
The head comes up. They sting.

Breathe water. Become river head to foot.
Hornets leave you alone then.[7]

See also chapter 55.

FIFTY-NINE

Translations of this chapter differ considerably. The present translation is unique in connecting restraint with *giving up one's own ideas.* All the versions, however, suggest that what is being spoken of here is the accumulation of a certain force within oneself, which confers to the individual a kind of capacity that is beyond ordinary understanding. No one can be a ruler (of

[7] Rumi, *We Are Three* (Athens, Georgia: Maypop Books, 1987), 42.

others or himself) without this mysterious capacity. This chapter is unusual and important, therefore, in referring to the cumulative effect or result in inner spiritual work. The luminous way in which Lao Tsu emphasizes the present moment of awareness may lead to a cheapened understanding along the lines of "living for the moment." This chapter corrects that possible misunderstanding and reminds us that there is also the need for long and persistent inner work.

SIXTY-THREE AND SIXTY-FOUR

Compare "Sufficient unto the day is the evil thereof" (Matthew 6:34). These two chapters deal with the art of living considered as the practice of giving one's best attention to the present moment with all its details. The sage is distinguished not only by *what* he does but by the attention he brings to life. Out of this art of living there can emerge great practical wisdom. We are being told, in short, that our lives are a reflection of the quality of our attention.

SIXTY-FIVE

In the beginning those who knew the Tao did not try to enlighten others, but kept it hidden.
They did not explain in words and concepts, or make moral precepts of that which can only be sensed and intuited. The wise do not pander to the "clever," who make mental representations out of sacred ideas and therefore imagine something is under-

stood when it is only named. This chapter, like almost all the text, resonates to the inner search as well: we are being advised, as it were, to keep our own cleverness from making the Way into merely mental information. I take this to be the central meaning of the famous opening of chapter 56:

> Those who know do not talk,
> Those who talk do not know.

Consider also: "Let not thy left hand know what thy right hand doeth" (Matthew 6:3). The way to great unity requires as well great and true separation — discrimination of essences and levels in both the outer and inner life. Compare also the restrictions against certain forms of "mixing" in the Judaic tradition.

SEVENTY-ONE

Plato tells us that the oracle at Delphi called Socrates the wisest of all men. "What in the world does the god mean?" asks Socrates. "What in the world is his riddle? For I know in my conscience that I am not wise in anything, great or small; then what in the world does he mean when he says I am wisest?" Socrates then proceeds to question citizens of Athens who have a reputation for wisdom — statesmen, scientists, artists, craftsmen — and is shocked to realize that no one else is any wiser than he. "The fact is that neither of us knows anything beautiful and good, but he thinks he does know when he doesn't and I don't know and don't think I do" (Apology, 21). Socrates' wisdom consists in the awareness that he is not wise.

This succinct chapter offers echoes of a truly momentous idea in the great spiritual traditions, expressed most paradoxically in the Mahayana Buddhist doctrine that *nirvana* (freedom) is *samsara* (slavery). *Nirvana* is the total awareness of *samsara*; freedom is the total awareness of slavery; knowledge is the total awareness of ignorance. Such awareness is not mere mental awareness, not merely the thought that one knows nothing or is enslaved. It is awareness as a tangible force and can carry with it the power of feeling and sensing that itself conducts a great liberating energy into the tissues of human life. Thus, in the Christian contemplative tradition, the most important factor in the inner life is remorse, "tears" in confrontation with one's own distance from God. This remorse opens the way for the grace or mercy of God to enter. It cannot be simulated; it must be genuine. This is the principal meaning of humility. "Blessed are they that mourn . . ." (Matthew 5:4).

SEVENTY-FOUR AND SEVENTY-FIVE

These chapters concern rulers who interfere too much, who impose their will upon the people. The true master of the people, and of the people in oneself, loves and cares for their life and they spontaneously return that love. Translators differ on the meaning of the term *executioner* in chapter 74. The general sense seems to be that one must destroy only that which is truly harmful to the state or to oneself and that this cannot be discerned without the authentic, impartial love for the whole that is the mark of the wise man, of the master.

SELECTED BIBLIOGRAPHY

Blakney, R. B. *The Way of Life: Lao Tzu.* New York: New American Library, 1955. Interestingly rendered in the form of English verse, which gives the text a more Westernized feeling and meaning. Introduction and notes offer useful associations with Western mystical writings.

Bynner, Witter. *The Way of Life according to Lao Tzu.* New York: Putnam Publishing Group, 1944. Departs significantly from a literal translation, yet succeeds in creating a valid philosophical poem of considerable strength.

Carus, Paul. *The Canon of Reason and Virtue.* LaSalle, Illinois: Open Court Publishing Company, 1964. Extracted from the pioneering translation originally published in 1898. Strong, insightful commentary. The translation is philosophical in successfully Westernized conceptual form.

Chan, Wing-Tsit. *The Way of Lao Tzu.* Indianapolis and New York: Bobbs-Merrill Co., 1963. Excellent scholarship together with a readable translation and an exceptionally helpful historical and philosophical introduction. Excellent notes. In general, a fine balance of academic thoroughness and human sensitivity.

Erkes, Eduard. *Ho-Shang-Kung's Commentary on Lao-tse.* Ascona, Switzerland: Press of Artibus Asiae, 1950. An important ancient commentary that offers fascinating perspectives on the meaning of the text.

Goddard, Dwight, and Bhikshu Wai-Tao. "Tao-Teh-King" in *A Buddhist Bible.* Edited by Dwight Goddard. New York: E. P. Dutton & Co., 1952. An admittedly interpretive translation that reads like a verse-by-verse summary-commentary. Very worthwhile in conjunction with more literal renderings; less reliable, but still interesting, on its own.

Lau, D. C. *Tao Te Ching.* Harmondsworth, England: Penguin Books, 1963. Scholarly and reliable with useful historical introduction and appendices.

Lin, Paul J. *A Translation of Lao Tzu's Tao Te Ching and Wang Pi's Commentary.* Ann Arbor: University of Michigan, Center for Chinese Studies, 1977. English translation of the text and of the oldest and most important commentary on it. Excellent historical and philosophical notes and an illuminating introduction dealing with the unique problems of translating from the Chinese text.

Lin Yutang. *The Wisdom of Laotse.* New York: Random House, 1948. Elegant and thoughtful translation including generous selections from Chuang Tsu as commentary. Very useful.

Maurer, Herrymon. *The Way of the Ways.* New York: Schocken Books, 1985. Renderings that reflect serious personal conviction and long experience with the text. Good references in the notes to other traditions, especially Christianity and Judaism in their mystical and contemplative aspects. Contemporary in a helpful way.

Mitchell, Stephen. *Tao Te Ching.* New York: Harper & Row, 1988. Many verses rendered with poetic beauty and a strong sense of the contemporary reader. Overall interpretation of the text seems to be from the perspective of "American Zen."

Rump, Ariane, with Wing-Tsit Chan. *Commentary on the Lao Tzu by Wang Pi*. Honolulu: University Press of Hawaii, 1979. English translation of the text and of the oldest and most important commentary on it. Extremely helpful and remarkably resonant philosophically.

Ta-Kao, Ch'u. *Tao Te Ching*. London: George Allen & Unwin Ltd., 1937. Not elegant, but solid and reliable.

Tao Te Ching. London, Santa Barbara, and New York: Concord Grove Press, 1983. One of the most interesting and sensitive modern versions.

Waley, Arthur. *The Way and Its Power*. London: George Allen & Unwin Ltd., 1934. Highly insightful and bold translation and commentary. Strongly recommended.

Wilhelm, Richard. *Tao Te Ching*. Translated by H. G. Ostwald. London and New York: Routledge & Kegan Paul, 1985. Vigorous and scholarly translation with serious philosophical commentary.

ABOUT THE TRANSLATORS

Gia-fu Feng was born in Shanghai in 1919, was educated in China, and came to the United States in 1947 to study comparative religion. He held a B.A. from Peking University and an M.A. from the University of Pennsylvania. He was the translator, with Jane English, of Chuang Tsu's *Inner Chapters*. He taught at the Esalen Institute, Big Sur, and directed the Stillpoint Foundation, a Taoist community in Manitou Springs, Colorado. Gia-fu Feng died in 1985.

Jane English, Ph.D. (Physics), in addition to collaborating on this translation of the *Tao Te Ching* with Gia-fu Feng, is a photographer whose black and white photographs of nature illustrate the 1972 edition of the book and its 1974 companion volume of Chuang Tsu's *Inner Chapters*. Since that time she has illustrated four other books and has also written and published two books, *Different Doorway: Adventures of a Caesarean Born* and *Childlessness Transformed: Stories of Alternative Parenting*.

ABOUT JACOB NEEDLEMAN

Jacob Needleman is the author and editor of ten books on philosophy and religion, including *Lost Christianity, The New Religions,* and *The Heart of Philosophy*. A professor of philosophy at San Francisco State University, he lives in San Francisco.